D0979335

5/21

THE HOPE
OF THE FAMILY

THE HOPE
OF THE FAMILY

*Dialogue with
Gerhard Cardinal Müller*

Edited by Carlos Granados

Translated by Michael J. Miller

IGNATIUS PRESS   SAN FRANCISCO

Original Spanish title:
La esperanza de la familia: Diálogo con el
Cardenal Gerhard-Ludwig Müller
© 2014 by Biblioteca de Autores Cristianos (BAC),
Madrid, Spain

Cover photo:
© get4net/pond5.com

Cover design by Enrique Javier Aguilar Pinto

© 2014 by Ignatius Press, San Francisco
All rights reserved
ISBN 978-1-62164-002-8
Library of Congress Control Number 2014946453
Printed in the United States of America ∞

CONTENTS

INTRODUCTION

We must thank BAC (Biblioteca de Autores Cristianos) for publishing this interview. It is to Cardinal Müller, however, that we owe our special thanks for the clarity with which he expressed himself about the problems that currently affect the Christian family.

The question about the participation of divorced and remarried Catholics in the sacraments will oblige us to rethink as a whole the place of the Sacrament of Matrimony in our Churches and, more broadly, the authenticity of the process of Christian initiation of our young people.

The sacraments are celebrations of faith in which the faith of believers blends with the traditional and communal faith of the Church. In the Sacrament of Matrimony, the Christian faithful, a man and a woman, celebrate with the

Church their faith in the love of God that is present and at work in them as members of the Church and coworkers of God in the multiplication of new members for mankind and for the Church of salvation.

Although there were times in which we could take the faith for granted, today we cannot, because we live in times of secularization and unbelief. We cannot ignore the existence of baptized persons who have no faith, who do not accept in its entirety the Christian view of marriage and family.

The main problem that we have in the Church concerning the family is not the small number of divorced and remarried persons who wish to approach the Eucharist in Holy Communion. The more serious problem that we have is the large number of baptized persons who marry civilly and the large number of baptized and sacramentally married persons who do not celebrate their wedding ceremony or live out their married life in accordance with Christian life and the teachings of the Church, as living icons of Christ's love for his Church, which is present and active in the world. Therefore, in our world, preparation for the Sacrament of Matrimony begins with the Christian conversion of adolescents and the religious and moral formation of young men and women.

It is possible that reading this little book will not be easy for some persons. Priests and Christian educators will do well to read it slowly and attentively and to reflect carefully on all that it contains. In it, Cardinal Müller gives us ideas and suggestions to help us reconsider, calmly and in depth, these questions within our tradition and the communion of the Church. With it, he does us a great service.

Madrid, June 29, 2014
Solemnity of Saint Peter and Saint Paul

Cardinal Fernando Sebastián
Archbishop Emeritus of Pamplona
Bishop Emeritus of Tudela

PREFACE BY THE EDITOR

"The hope of the family". The possessive case gives rise to various interpretations: a hope for the family, a hope that is based on the family, or even a hope that is the family itself. The purpose of this little book is to address the question that the Holy Father posed by convoking an Extraordinary Synod on the Family scheduled for October 2014, the question of the "pastoral challenges of the family". In order to do this, we have tried to travel a path by means of the questions we have posed to the cardinal prefect of the Congregation for the Doctrine of the Faith: the *pathway of hope* and not, primarily, the pathway of problems. The family, we might say, is in the first place the solution, not the problem. Hence the title selected refers to the fact that the family, the domestic church, is a source of hope and that it clearly needs to be strengthened in its mission, in other words, to go back to remembering what it is: "Family, be what you are."

The cardinal prefect of the CDF, Gerhard Müller, welcomed the idea of a dialogue about the family. The text basically compiles what emerged from the dialogue that the editor-in-chief of BAC, Father Carlos Granados, had with His Eminence in his office at the Congregation for the Doctrine of the Faith last month, in June 2014. The text was then revised by the latter. The question about the family arose and was formulated, obviously, within the context of the upcoming synod on the family. But it needed to be placed also in a wider context, in which the urgent questions do not obscure the background and the depth of the topic.

The idea of this dialogue sprang from a pastoral concern to make more comprehensible to the Christian faithful the meaning of what is heard and remarked these days about the upcoming synod (often in the media with little real information). The words of the prefect of the Congregation for the Doctrine of the Faith illuminate the framework within which today's questions about the family emerge; an attentive reading of them will make clear that the faith is the true light that brings the problems back to their true center.

The BAC wishes to thank Cardinal Müller for approving our project, for the trust that he showed at every moment, and for taking the time to conduct the interview and then to revise the text in its entirety.

Carlos Granados, Editor-in-chief
Biblioteca de Autores Cristianos

THE HOPE OF THE FAMILY

Dialogue with
Gerhard Cardinal Müller

Question: With enormous clear-sightedness, Pope Francis convoked an extraordinary synod on the family entitled "Pastoral Challenges of the Family in the Context of Evangelization". This is a real opportunity to address the challenges that our contemporary world poses to the family. What are these challenges? The first challenge seems to be the fact that young people no longer marry. There are those who say that this will be the real challenge for the synod on the family. In a romantic society, characterized by individuals who are extremely fragile emotionally, the trustworthiness of love has been called into question, and with

In the following pages, the questions of the interviewer, Father Carlos Granados García, editor-in-chief of BAC, will be printed in italics and introduced by "*Question*"; this will distinguish them from the cardinal prefect's answers, which will be in roman type, preceded by "*Cardinal Müller*".

it the value of the promise of "forever". Young people who face marriage encounter difficulties as they try to "believe in love". Love has become so fluid that it seems to have little strength to serve as a serious basis for planning a family. Young engaged couples, in fact, find it hard to believe in the soundness of the institution: What message should we convey to them? How can we foster hope in young people?

Cardinal Müller: It is obvious that the challenges posed by today's highly secularized world are enormous. On the one hand, in some traditionally Christian countries, we observe a progressive loss of the sense of the faith. At the same time, in many other places, the Christian religion has been reduced to a set of values, ideas, or social activities, thus losing what is essential and basic in the faith experience: the real encounter with Jesus Christ, the Son of God, and the total renewal of man in an eschatological perspective. Specifically, Christian marriage as a sacrament can be understood in its true significance only when approached from a christological and eschatological point of view.

Marriage is not simply living together with another person: it is a definitive decision within the framework of the relationship of Jesus Christ, the Bridegroom, with his Bride, the Church. As Pope Francis says so appropriately in his apostolic exhortation *Evangelii gaudium*, inventing a Spanish neologism, Christ *primerea*; he goes ahead of us and gets there first. From the creation of the world, God wished to say in Christ that his decision with regard to us, his children, was definitive and radical. That is why God willed that marriage should be this intimate, exclusive union between one man and one woman: this union is the source from which the family emerges and the criterion by which to appreciate it. In this regard, the Holy Father recently said that all marriages are ordered and inherently tend to be fruitful: children have their origin in spousal love. In his homily at the morning Mass celebrated in the chapel of *Casa Santa Marta* on June 2, the pope also recalled with some humor a contemporary situation that has a terribly tragic side: we mean the many couples who, instead of having children, prefer to keep a dog, a cat, or some other pet. Because they act this way, many married couples renounce the personal reciprocity that gives rise to the relationship with children, which is the fulfillment and the perfection of the conjugal love they profess.

I venture to say that the emotional formation of today's young people is one of the most serious problems we have to confront at the moment. Pastors observe with great concern that many young people turn their backs on the way of life proposed by the Church. Many of them refuse to live out and to enjoy their love in total fidelity, in an indissoluble marriage: in fact, we could say that the idea of commitment frightens them. Consequently, they understand sexuality as a mere pleasure, not as a great opportunity to receive and to communicate life within a community of love. They refuse to bring about a communion of life and love with the beloved person. Basically, I think, these young people are nothing but a vivid example of the serious difficulty that our world has in understanding the true dimension of human life as a communion. In a doggedly individualistic and subjectivist world, marriage is not perceived as an opportunity offered to a human being to achieve fulfillment by sharing in love. Someone will have to proclaim anew the true God, who is a Trinity of love! We will have to proclaim the God of revelation who calls us all to share in his own relational being. We will have to emphasize that this sharing in the divine life is not reserved for a few select individuals but has been offered to us all, whether single or married. Above all, we will have to explain that this was the great "wedding gift" that God gave to humanity, by means of the Incarnation of the Word and the outpouring of the Holy Spirit.

Remote preparation for marriage, that is, from childhood and adolescence on, ought to be one of the first pastoral priorities in education. A child who discovers that he is unconditionally loved as a son will recognize himself in adolescence as someone who feels impelled to love another person and, finally, in adulthood, after recognizing his spousal dimension, as someone who discovers that his love is fruitful. But I insist that the proximate or immediate preparation for marriage will be ineffective if we do not educate Catholics from birth about the personal and affective dimension of the person. Only in this way will we succeed in harmonizing the basic dimensions of human existence: the person, sociability, fruitfulness, responsibility, education, and communion. This is the foundation for a thorough understanding of matrimony.

Young people have the right to experience from the first moment of their lives the things that only the family can offer: I am referring to the confidence and balance that result from the fact of being accepted and welcomed unconditionally by their own parents. There is no better way of laying the groundwork for true hope in young people. For them, their parents are the first representatives of God's love. They mediate the confidence that results from knowing that they are welcomed and cherished by the hands of their Creator, who loved us even before we were conceived. To put it in more theological language, through their participation in the common priesthood of all the faithful, our own parents are priestly representatives of this confidence, love, and unconditional acceptance of our human existence.

Question: Young people today, as we said, experience great difficulty in making a promise, such as a matrimonial vow, which demands fidelity "forever". Pope Francis reminded us in his apostolic exhortation Evangelii gaudium *that "the individualism of our postmodern and globalized era favors a lifestyle which weakens the development and stability of personal relationships and distorts family bonds" (no. 67). In this context, how are we to understand the "forever" of marriage? Is it a limit and a reason not to marry, or is it a manifestation of the great hope that husband and wife have when they contract marriage?*

Cardinal Müller: This "forever" is clearly rooted in the "once and for all" of the sacrifice of Jesus Christ on the Cross, who gave up his own life for us. To give one's life is, so to speak, the symbol of love, inasmuch as it is not a vague sentiment but a reality: fulfilling oneself through an act of self-surrender. The heart of love is God's surrender of himself for our sake. We were freed from ourselves, from selfishness, when we were created for the triune God who lives in love, in the relationship of the Father with the Son in the Holy Spirit. Therefore, being relational is and will always be fundamental to our existence. It is impossible to live in isolation or wrapped up in ourselves! Life acquires meaning only when it becomes a concrete gift of self to someone else: in our everyday routine, day by day. In a special way, this meaning is found in the mystery of matrimony: it is transformed into the privileged place in which to experience a form of unconditional and definitive self-giving that gives meaning to our lives. Nevertheless, this commitment, which is so thrilling and beautiful, also has a limitation: namely, it cannot be achieved by our own efforts. Without the humble acknowledgment of our own limitations and without the sincere offer of the forgiveness we have received from God, it is not possible to maintain a "forever". I think that behind many families that are broken or patched together, with different "fathers" or "mothers" or with only "mothers" or "fathers", there is basically a lack of understanding of something that we used to think was obvious.

In my opinion, the main object of the next synod should be to facilitate the recovery of the sacramental idea of marriage and family, thus conferring on the young people who are ready to begin a marital journey or on those who have already started one the courage they need. Basically, this is a matter of telling them that they are not alone on this journey, that the Church, always a mother, is accompanying them and will accompany them. Certainly, this task would be impossible to accomplish if we relied merely on the publication of a few specialized books or articles. We cannot forget the power of the witness of marriages that do not break up! These marriages, with which we are all acquainted, these happy, fulfilled couples who have achieved a full life, are, more often than not unconsciously, the privileged witnesses of the truth of human love.

The Holy Father often speaks to us about the reality of poverty, embodied in the poor of the Third and Fourth World, who are "marginalized", relegated to the so-called "peripheries of life". Among them are also the children who have to grow up without their own parents, the so-called "orphans of divorce". They are, perhaps, the poorest in the world: these are the abandoned children not only in Third World countries, but also here, in Europe, in North America, in the wealthiest countries. These "orphans of divorce", sometimes surrounded by many belongings and with a lot of money at their disposal, are the poorest of the poor, since they have many material goods but are lacking the most basic thing: the solicitous love of parents who renounce themselves for their sake. This is because only spiritual goods, and not material ones, enable us to mature and to reach adulthood safely.

You have pointed out the great difficulty of living out the promise of "forever". Certainly, the doctrine about the indissolubility of marriage is today one of the most misunderstood doctrines in our secularized environments. In places where the Christian faith has become irrelevant and has lost its fundamental reasons for being, the fact of belonging to the Church in a conventional way, without any requirements, is not enough to guide a person's concrete choices in life or to offer reliable support to those who are experiencing a marital crisis. The same thing happens, certainly, in the vocation to the priesthood or the religious life.

Many people wonder: How will I ever be able to bind myself to one person for my whole life? Who can tell what will happen in twenty or thirty years of marriage or how I will have changed? Is a definitive bond with just one person really possible? The negative experiences of so many people reinforce the skepticism of many others about such a demanding and radical decision as Christian married life.

On the other hand, I would like to emphasize that recent surveys taken among Catholic young people show that the idea of fidelity between a husband and a wife, founded in the order of creation, continues to be fascinating for them, too. Even if they say they "believe" in divorce, most of them aspire to have a faithful, lasting relationship that corresponds to the spiritual and moral nature of marriage. Moreover, we must not forget that indissoluble marriage has an anthropological value of the first order: it removes a person from the arbitrariness and tyranny of feelings and moods; it helps him to confront personal difficulties and to overcome painful experiences; above all, it protects the children. This is why we say that love is something more than a sentiment or an instinct. In its very essence, it is a form of dedication and self-surrender. In marital love, two persons say to one another consciously and voluntarily: You are so important to me, you are so unique to me, that I want to be with you only, forever! The word of the Lord, "What God has joined together, let no man put asunder", corresponds to the promise that every couple exchanges: "I, N., take you, N., to be my [lawful wedded] husband/wife." This foundation that makes hope possible is what must be communicated once again to young people so that they, with renewed courage, might be able to face the great challenge of "forever". Nevertheless, I insist: in the present cultural context, it proves to be very difficult to understand these postulates without a faith that has been personally accepted and lived out.

Question: "Postmodern individualism" has resulted in a privatization of the family, with disastrous consequences. The family has ceased to be relevant among the general public and even in pastoral programs within the Church; it has been relegated to the sphere

*of subjectivity, of what goes on "behind closed doors".
What is the cause of this privatizing trend? What are
the consequences of it? How can the Church help the
family to become a true sort of "social capital"?*

Cardinal Müller: Yes, clearly, this is one of the
reasons for the failure of so many families: they
are isolated in themselves, self-contained, as an
extension of the "privatization" that the individual is led to practice in our capitalistic and
radically individualistic societies. Only when
one individual opens himself to another is he
capable of successfully forming with that person
a new reality that transcends the individual: I am
referring to the reality of marriage, the primary
and original cell of the entire social organism.
Therefore, I find it so necessary that Christian
families, true domestic churches, be integrated
once again into the universal Church through
the parishes or through the movements that are
active within them, because ecclesial communities are a symbol of the great family that God
desires. In major cities, pastors ought to give
priority to the establishment of connections and
bridges between some Christian families and

others, thus revitalizing their parishes as places of encounter in which to live out and celebrate the faith.

We ought to keep more clearly in mind the fact that our society exalts individual rights to the point where they become detrimental. Deliberately, in a clear attempt to manipulate and dominate, the selfish behaviors of individuals or of small, self-contained groups are favored and privileged. On the other hand, society overlooks or even persecutes everything that contributes to the common good, to genuine solidarity, to communion, to sharing one's own life with others.

Therefore, in order to save modern civilization, it would be necessary to renew it, starting with the family as the domestic church. We Christians, too, should understand that the Church is not made up exclusively of persons— yes, of course there are persons in her—but also of families! I say, we should reclaim a "Church of families". Just as in the different countries of the world, the pilgrim Church exists in one place or another, in Spain too, and is a particular Church, in the context of a particular language, history, and culture, so too it happens with the particular characteristics of the Church as they are experienced in a specific family. And all these families are integrated into the one Church of Christ. No two families are alike, yet thousands of families can meet in an event attended by a huge crowd—for example, in the World Meeting of Families that was held in Madrid in recent years—and recognize that they are all a gift from God. This diversity, which is an essential part of the Christian paradigm that the institution of the family embodies so sublimely, is the best example of the unity that the Spirit brings about!

This is why contemporary theology situates marriage in an ecclesiological context. In light of a fuller anthropology with greater emphasis on personal responsibility and communication, the Second Vatican Council describes it as one of the essential sacramental acts of the Church, defining it as "the domestic church, [in which] the parents should, by their word and example, be the first preachers of the faith to their children; they should encourage them in the vocation which is proper to each of them" (LG 11).

Question: It seems that another major challenge of the family today, insofar as its meaning is concerned, is of a cultural sort. I am referring to the sexual revolution of the 1960s, which, in order to change the way in which people understood sexuality, spread an ideology that weakens the understanding of the family in comparison to other ostensible family models, making it difficult for persons to experience authentically what their hearts desire: a true family. How can this challenge be addressed? What cultural challenge does this paradigm shift involve?

Cardinal Müller: The sexual revolution destroyed many really important anthropological fundamentals. No wonder, because lurking behind this phenomenon is nihilism, in other words, a philosophy that empties everything human of its transcendent contents. Nowadays it is not uncommon to deny the existence of God or, at least, to declare with utter indifference that one is agnostically neutral. As a result, the anthropological concept that is offered to our young people puts at the center of reality a man and a woman devoid of all transcendent meaning, reduced, as it were, to their animal instincts, making use of their freedom without any prior moral criterion. When life lacks transcendent meaning, human existence is reduced to material things, and the only reason for being or existing is pleasure, especially sexual pleasure, money, prestige, or health. These are the new idols that have replaced God as man's point of reference; they have made self-sacrificing love, altruism, or love of neighbor almost impossible. There is a lot of talk about love, but it is understood as a subjective feeling of pleasure, which can occasionally be shared with another person of the other sex or even of the same sex.

I think that in the present situation there is an urgent need to offer to everyone a well-founded reflection on human existence in its indivisible unity of body and soul, starting with an adequate anthropology. It is necessary to give a reason for our hope! We ought to invite everyone to integrate sexuality correctly into this novel interpretation of reality.

We also should reinterpret a perennial truth and propose it again in a new language adapted to today's world: the person in his relationship with God. The God who is love gives me his grace so that I may be fulfilled in love. God delivers himself up so that I might have existence and find that the center of my life is "to be for others" and not "to be in order to satisfy my own whims", by concentrating on myself. Maybe we will have to be bolder and proclaim that the only alternative to egocentrism is theocentrism!

Question: Nevertheless, in the context of these challenges, it is worthwhile to dwell on the relation between the crisis of the family and the crisis of faith that Pope Benedict XVI already pointed out at the start of the synod on the new evangelization. Pope Francis, in his speech on the occasion of the ad limina *visit of the Spanish bishops, alluded to this same factor when he declared that the family is the place "where the faith is molded and lived". The American scholar Mary Eberstadt has made it clear that the relation between secularization and the family is a two-way street: it is not just that the crisis of the presence of God in human life has caused a crisis in the family, but also that the crisis of the family has caused a crisis in our awareness of God: the more common divorce becomes, the more difficult it is to believe in God's love and that it can be the foundation of one's life. But what does this relation between the crisis of God and the crisis of the family mean? Does it not perhaps imply, in a positive sense, that "to build up the family" is already "to evangelize"? To dwell on an example and a concrete application of this question: How could the family and Christian initiation be more deeply united? What would that involve? What advantages would it have?*

Cardinal Müller: It is not difficult to see the close connection between secularization and the crisis of the family. This relation is very clear and palpable. Through the Magisterium, we know that the family is a "domestic church" (LG 11, FC 21). Moreover, we have all clearly experienced the fact that our parents are the first representatives of God's love and that therefore we can be confident that God exists.

The prescription for emerging from the crisis described here in broad strokes may be to begin with a correct analysis. Every good analysis is a *sine qua non* condition for a new synthesis, which in turn enables us to overcome the crisis that prompted that analysis. By the way, we observe that most religious vocations come from families in the lay movements or from lively parishes that understand that they are parts of the great family of God. It is true that adult converts to Christianity are a recent ecclesial phenomenon, but even though their strong faith may even be enviable in comparison to the faith of others who were born in a more favorable environment, they too, as new Christians, quickly notice the need to give witness to their own families. In the end, it always comes down to the family. And this makes me think that the individual is always called to grow in the family, not just biologically, but also from the intellectual, emotional, and above all spiritual point of view. However, and as a general rule, this last-mentioned aspect is accomplished, not through books or knowledge, but rather through persons and their living witness. So we see that there is no contradiction between intellectual and spiritual growth, because man is a rational animal who must understand what he believes—a faculty of reason that sheds light on the faith and a faith that illuminates reason, as Pope Benedict XVI insistently reminded us.

In all this we must keep in mind that according to Christianity, the relation that is basic to everything is personal and consists of witness: only later do we reflect with the intellect on what we have experienced and on the things that have awakened in us a desire for fullness. Classical philosophy formulates this as *fides quarens intellectum*, faith seeking understanding, not vice versa.

Question: From what you have just told us, we could conclude, reducing it to a slogan, that the more fragile the family, the more difficult it is to believe in God? In other words, that somehow witness to God in the world is thus weakened?

Cardinal Müller: Well, in itself the increase in broken marriages does not necessarily imply a denial of God's existence. The human judgment that God exists is the prerequisite for the faith, it is part of the *preambula fidei*. Nevertheless, the ultimate knowledge of God requires the experience of "familiarity" with him: without family, there is no such experience of familiarity with God that is basic for faith! I insist that this correlation is not automatic. Therefore, we cannot state categorically that because a child grows up in a broken family, as an adult he will be an atheist. We all know of counterexamples, too: staunch believers who grew up in a broken family and staunch atheists who come from deeply Christian families. But we cannot deny, either, that living within a Christian family is the best environment. Yes, it is much better! The faith, in the context of a normal life, has more opportunities to put down roots and to develop harmoniously with the other personal dimensions. Praying as a family, going to Mass together ... considered in this way, the Christian faith has more of a chance to take root.

Question: Faced with the difficulties of the family, which are certainly serious, has the Church been able to give an adequate response? Many times families sense a certain remoteness of the Church when they present their problems: many priests do not know what to do about them; even the ecclesial activities that are offered are frequently not designed for the family but for individuals. On the other hand, the enormous efforts made in recent years for the pastoral care of young people (which are often "recreational" instead of "teaching life skills") have not led to any development in the pastoral care of families. Has something been missing? What pastoral challenge is presented within the Church?

Cardinal Müller: In recent decades we have made a great effort to organize pastoral activities for the various categories, ages, and groups of the faithful, yet, being victims of modern individualism, we have been unable to offer authentic familial pastoral care for a family that is, on the other hand, "sick with selfishness".

The individualistic family is another typically modern category: how many families languish because they are confined to themselves! I recall, as a counterexample, our family reunions long ago or many of our homes where spouses often lived with their respective parents along with their own children. The dynamic typical of modern life brings with it another sort of family, one that is atomized, and this is precisely why it is necessary to strengthen two dimensions: the family as an organism or a home and the family itself being open to other families, where its members grow and are enriched thanks to friendship with others.

With regard to this question, Pope Francis urges us not to give in to our "throw-away" culture, whereby many families reject the enrichment of sharing their time with others, including their elders, who are considered an insupportable, expendable burden. What Christianity proposes has always been a "culture of welcoming", especially of the most needy: in this case, welcoming grandparents will be in the long run a source of incalculable riches for the young couple who have dared to go against the trend.

On the other hand, it is necessary also to make an effort to understand the different historical moments of families; after all, we want to offer a pastoral approach that truly has an effect on them. It is very important to be attentive to the different ages of family members or to the stage in its life: a family that revolves around a young couple is one thing, while a young family with children is another, and this is not the same as a large family with children including some

who are already married or a family with sick
or disabled members. There are different family
circumstances that must be taken into account
when one is making a pastoral plan.

As for pastoral practices, in my former arch-
diocese of Regensburg, it is quite common to
offer Eucharistic liturgies for families with very
young children. This seems to me to be a
very good idea. We no longer talk about "a children's Mass" but, rather, more accurately, about
"a family Mass" since the attempt to introduce
a child to the faith is useless and even counterproductive if this is done behind the back of his
family. Everyone should be at a family Mass:
grandparents, parents, and children. Likewise, it
is necessary to carry out a "family catechesis" in
our parishes, designed by and for families, to the
extent that that is possible. No doubt this is the
type of initiative that should be fostered.

*Question: One specific point of this ecclesial response
has to do with the formation of priests. Does it
respond to the urgency of the challenges of the family? Sometimes in seminaries marriage is an incidental
academic subject; shouldn't something be done about*

this? Wouldn't that also strengthen the identity of priests, their fatherhood?

Cardinal Müller: That is quite clear, isn't it? We need to do something about the formation of priests, so that they are able to respond adequately to the new challenges described earlier. They should be better prepared to minister to families as such and not just to individuals. They should carry out a more comprehensive, multidisciplinary approach to the family, not only in terms of canon law. By the way, we should keep in mind the great wealth that is to be found in the various theological focuses on the family: *dogmatic theology* considers Christian marriage from the formal perspective of its "sacramentality" and of its essential qualities, such as indissolubility, monogamy, and fruitfulness, which is connected with the willingness to educate the children in the faith. *Moral theology* deals with marriage above all from the perspective of an anthropology of sexuality and of responsible parenthood. *Canon law* considers it from the viewpoint of its legitimate establishment and its pathologies, with the problems that arise when matrimonial consent is vitiated or hindered by various circumstances. For its part, *pastoral theology* studies it under the aspect of promoting it, so that the plan for a family arrives at the right destination: here, too, the question of how to treat those who are divorced as well as divorced and remarried Catholics comes into play. All these aspects are important, as is *spiritual theology*, if we are talking about introducing the family to Christian prayer. How important it is that prayer, Bible reading, and reading the lives of the saints should be part of the shared components of family life!

How many challenges the pastoral care of families poses! We must show young families a way of living and acting again as Christians in our times: not only during Mass, when receiving the sacraments, or acting in the public life of the Church, but also in the formation and organization of the family structure itself. After that it will be necessary to put it into practice, mainly with the help offered by the witness of many, many families who regularly follow the practices of their Christian faith: morning or night prayer, periodic examination of conscience, meditation together, visits to shrines, participation in associations or in popular devotions. Isn't this precisely the beginning of a new evangelization of the family?

Question: Public opinion in recent months has been very concerned about the problem of divorced and remarried persons. It has gone so far as to call into question the criterion established in Familiaris consortio, *which in number 84 says: "The Church reaffirms her practice, which is based upon Sacred Scripture, of not admitting to Eucharistic Communion divorced persons who have remarried. They are unable to be admitted thereto from the fact that their state and condition of life objectively contradict that union of love between Christ and the Church which is signified and effected by the Eucharist. Besides this, there is another special pastoral reason: if these people were admitted to the Eucharist, the faithful would be led into error and confusion regarding the Church's teaching about the indissolubility of marriage." Starting from a certain interpretation of Scripture, patristic tradition, and magisterial documents, some recent commentaries have hinted that it is time to propose an updated version of* Familiaris consortio. *What position should we take with regard to this? Is it possible to hope that there might be a change of doctrine in this matter? But above all (to formulate the problem more clearly and proactively): Is there any concrete way to accommodate divorced persons who have entered a new civil union?*

Cardinal Müller: Not even an ecumenical council can change the doctrine of the Church, because her Founder, Jesus Christ, entrusted the faithful preservation of his teachings and doctrine to the apostles and their successors. The Gospel of Matthew says: "Go and teach all people everything that I commanded you" (cf. Mt 28:19–20), which is nothing if not a definition of the "deposit of the faith" (*depositum fidei*) that the Church has received and cannot change. Therefore the doctrine of the Church will never be the sum total of a few theories worked out by a handful of theologians, however ingenious they may be, but rather the profession of our faith in revelation, nothing more and nothing less than the Word of God entrusted to the heart—the interiority—and the lips—the proclamation—of his Church.

We have an elaborate, structured doctrine about marriage, all of it based on the words of Jesus himself, which must be presented in its entirety. We encounter it in the Gospels and in other places in the New Testament, especially in the words of Saint Paul in the First Letter to the Corinthians and in Romans. We also rely on tradition, with many writings and reflections of the Fathers of the Church, such as those of Saint Augustine. These are joined by the particular development that Scholasticism and the Magisterium made in the Councils of Florence and Trent. Lastly, a final stage in the progressive exposition of dogma is magnificently expressed for us in *Lumen gentium* and, above all, in *Gaudium et spes* (nos. 47–51), which are a complete synthesis that the Second Vatican Council made of the Church's entire doctrine on marriage, including the question about divorce also.

In this regard, the Church cannot allow divorce in the case of a sacramental marriage that has been contracted and consummated. This is the dogma of the Church. I insist: the absolute indissolubility of a valid marriage is no mere doctrine; rather, it is a divine dogma defined by the Church. In the case of a *de facto* break-up of a valid marriage, another civil "marriage" is not permissible. Otherwise, we would be facing a contradiction, because if the earlier union, the "first" marriage, or, more precisely, *the* marriage, really is a marriage, the other later union is not a "marriage". In this regard, I think we are playing with words when we speak about a first and a second "marriage". A second marriage is possible only when one's legitimate spouse has died or when the previous marriage has been declared invalid, whereby the preceding bond has been dissolved. Otherwise, we are dealing with what is called an "impediment of the bond".

There are many respectable authors, renowned for their prestige in theology and canon law, who at present warn about the danger of simplifying or even adulterating these teachings. In this connection, I want to emphasize that in 1994, then-Cardinal Joseph Ratzinger, prefect of the congregation over which I now preside, with the approval of then-Pope Saint John Paul II, had to intervene expressly in order to reject a hypothesis that had appeared (the one that you set forth in your question).

At the root of the question you pose, and beyond any apparent theological dispute, we must keep in mind that we are addressing a problem that casts doubt on the fact that it is necessary for the Church always to remain faithful to the doctrine of Jesus, whose words in this regard are absolutely clear.

This does not prevent us, however, from speaking, as we must, about the problem of the validity of many marriages in the present context of secularization. We have all attended a wedding at which you could not tell whether the intention of the couple contracting marriage really was to "do what the Church does" in the rite of matrimony! In theory, we all know the criteria or classical conditions for being able to contract marriage; especially that the will to consent not be vitiated but rather should be free and that there be sufficient personal maturity. Nevertheless, this current situation described earlier makes us reflect, and, as pastors, we are worried about the fact that many people who contract marriage are formally Christians, since they have received baptism, but are not practicing the Christian faith at all; not just liturgically, but also existentially.

Benedict XVI issued an insistent call to reflect on the great challenge posed by baptized nonbelievers. Consequently, the Congregation for the Doctrine of the Faith took up this concern of the pope and set a good number of its theologians and other collaborators to work on the problem of the relation between explicit and implicit faith. What happens to a marriage when even implicit faith is lacking in it? It is certain that when implicit faith is absent, even though it was celebrated *libre et recte* [with free consent and with the proper form], it could be that it was invalid. It leads us to think that besides the classical criteria for declaring the invalidity of a marriage, it is necessary to reflect more on the case in which the spouses exclude the sacramentality of marriage. At the moment we are still in the process of working, with calm but persistent reflection, on this matter. I think that it would not be good to propose hasty conclusions, since we have not yet found a solution, but this does not prevent me from pointing out that in our congregation we are making great efforts to give a correct answer to the problem posed by implicit faith in the contracting parties.

Question: So that if the subject were to exclude the sacramentality of marriage, just as if one were to exclude children, for example, at the moment of the wedding, this could also make the contracted marriage null. Is this what is being studied ...

Cardinal Müller: Faith is an essential part of the sacrament. Nevertheless, we have to clarify the juridical question posed by the invalidity of the sacrament because of an obvious lack of faith. A famous canonist, Eugène Corecco, used to say that the root of the problem is specifying the degree of faith necessary to bring about sacramentality. The classical doctrine assumed a minimalist position, requiring a merely implicit intention: "to do what the Church does". Corecco added that in today's globalized, multicultural, and secularized world, where the faith is something that cannot simply be taken for granted, it becomes necessary to require a more explicit faith of the contracting parties, if we really want to save Christian marriage. Nevertheless, I emphasize again that this question is still being studied. To establish a valid and universal criterion in this regard is not a trivial question. In the first place, because persons are constantly developing, in matters pertaining both to the knowledge they acquire over the years and also to their faith life. Learning and faith are not static data! Sometimes at the moment when marriage is contracted, a person was not a believer; but it is also possible that a conversion process took place in his life, through which he experienced a *sanatio ex posteriori* [a "healing" or validation after the fact] of what was a serious defect of consent at the moment when it was given.

I want to insist, however, that when we are dealing with a valid sacramental marriage, in no way is it possible to dissolve that matrimonial bond: neither the pope nor any other bishop has the authority to do so, because this reality is not their concern but, rather, belongs to God.

Question: In this same context, there is talk about giving spouses the option to "redo their lives". What are the underlying assumptions of this question? Is it a good approach to the problem? Most importantly: If the revelation of God was constantly bound up, both in the Old and in the New Testament, with the nuptial mystery and with a certain concept of the reality of marriage, what implications would that have for the faith? Within this same framework, it has also been said that the love between Christian spouses can "die". I ask myself: Can a Christian really use this expression? Is it possible for the love between two persons united by the Sacrament of Matrimony to die?

Cardinal Müller: These theories are radically wrong, because they refer terminology that may be true about the life of the spouses to the life of their love. One cannot declare a marriage defunct with the excuse that the love between the spouses has "died". Contrary to what many people claim today, in a not disinterested way, love is something more than a feeling. Love is the will that a person has to share his life with another and, above all, to give himself to her. Marital indissolubility does not depend on human feelings, whether they are permanent or transitory. This property of marriage was willed by God himself. The Lord has become involved in a marriage between a man and a woman, and for this reason the bond exists and originates in God. This is the difference.

The proposal to which you refer is in itself yet another expression of the grave secularization of marriage. But basically it is an instance of "begging the question" (*petitio principii*). In reality, only the death of a spouse dissolves the bond of a sacramental marriage. And I am not referring to death in a metaphorical sense. The reason for this is that the marriage is not only a merely human reality; it is a transformed human reality. The kind of marriage desired by Christ is a sacrament; it is a visible representation of the transforming grace that has created a new reality that did not exist before. In this regard, we must consider that the indelible character of baptism, confirmation, or priestly ordination does not disappear, either, when the Catholic who has received the sacrament distances himself from the Church or from his priestly commitments. Theological tradition speaks in this connection about a "quasi-sacramental character" in matrimony, because a person is permitted to contract a new marriage after the death of the spouse, but not while the spouse is alive.

In its intrinsic supernatural reality, marriage includes three goods: the good of exclusive, personal, reciprocal fidelity (the *bonum fidei*), the good of welcoming children and educating them to know God (the *bonum prolis*), and the good of the indissolubility or indestructibility of the bond, the permanent foundation of which is the indissoluble union of Christ and the Church, which is sacramentally represented by the marriage (the *bonum sacramenti*). This is why, although a limited abrogation of the physical communion of life and love is possible, the so-called "separation from bed and board", for a Christian it is not lawful to contract a new marriage while the first spouse is alive, because the legitimately contracted bond is perpetual. The indissoluble matrimonial bond corresponds in a way to the character (*res et sacramentum*) imprinted in baptism, confirmation, and holy orders.

Question: In this context there has been much talk also about the importance of "mercy". This is certainly a decisive theme in divine revelation. The God of the Old Testament reveals himself as "abounding in mercy and faithfulness". Then in Jesus he manifests to us fully this merciful face of God. When applying this terminology to the topic of marriage, nevertheless, commentators seem to forget that this terminology is anchored in "faithfulness to the covenant", and mercy is therefore mentioned precisely as a reason for the contrary, in other words, to justify the fact that fidelity to the matrimonial promise is broken. What should be said in this regard? Can mercy be interpreted as a way of "making exceptions" to the moral law? Since today's society has secularized love, shouldn't the prophetic voice of the Church perhaps be an expression of mercy?

Cardinal Müller: Saint Thomas Aquinas said that mercy is precisely the fulfillment of justice, since God thereby justifies and renews his creature man (cf. *Summa Theologiae,* I, q. 21, a. 3). Therefore, it should never be used as a justification to suspend or invalidate the commandments and the sacraments. To do that would be a crude manipulation of genuine mercy and, therefore, a vain attempt to justify our own indifference toward God and man.

If we turn to the Gospel, we observe how Jesus, in his dialogue with the Pharisees concerning divorce, also has recourse to the two terms "divorce" and "mercy" (cf. Mt 19:3–12). Precisely in this passage he accuses the Pharisees of "hardness of heart", of being unmerciful, since in their tortured interpretation of the Law they have concluded that Moses supposedly granted permission for them to dismiss their wives. Jesus reminds them that God's mercy is contrary to our human weakness. God grants us his grace so that we can be faithful. This is the true purpose of God's mercy. God even forgives such a serious sin as adultery; nevertheless, he does not allow another marriage that would call into doubt an existing sacramental marriage, since the latter expresses God's faithfulness. To appeal in the way just described to an allegedly absolute "mercy" of God is nothing but wordplay, which does not help to clarify the terms of the problem. In reality, I venture to say that, instead, it obscures the ability to perceive the depths of authentic divine mercy.

I observe with a certain amazement the use by some theologians, once again, of the same reasoning about mercy as an excuse for promoting the admission of divorced and civilly remarried persons to the sacraments. Their initial premise is that Jesus himself practiced solidarity with those who suffer, offering them his merciful love, and therefore mercy is the special sign that characterizes all authentic pastoral care. There is some truth to this. Nevertheless, the "principle of mercy" is very weak when it is transformed into the one and only valid theological-sacramental argument. The whole sacramental order is precisely the work of divine mercy, but it cannot be revoked by appealing to the same principle that supports it. On the contrary: an erroneous reference to mercy entails the serious danger of trivializing the very image of God, by implying that God would not be free but would be forced to forgive. God never tires of offering us his mercy: the problem is that we tire of asking for it by humbly acknowledging our own sinfulness, as Pope Francis has insistently reminded us during the first year and a half of his pontificate.

The scriptural evidence shows us that, besides mercy, holiness and justice are also part of the mystery of God. If these divine attributes are obscured and the reality of sin is trivialized, it would make no sense, either, to mediate God's mercy for people. Thus it is understandable that Jesus, after treating the adulterous woman with great mercy, should tell her as an expression of his love: "Go and do not sin again" (Jn 8:11). God's mercy, therefore, is not a dispensation from God's commandments and the teachings of the Church. Quite the contrary: God, by his infinite mercy, grants us the grace and strength to obey his commandments fully and thus the ability to reestablish in us, after the fall, his perfect image as our Heavenly Father.

Question: Another thing being proposed here, obviously, is the relation between the Sacrament of the Eucharist and the Sacrament of Matrimony. What can you tell us in this regard? How can the relation between the two sacraments be understood?

Cardinal Müller: Eucharistic Communion is the expression of a personal and communal relationship with Jesus Christ. It expresses for Catholics, unlike our Protestant brethren and in keeping with the tradition of the Church, the perfect union between Christology and ecclesiology. Therefore, I cannot have a personal relationship with Christ and with his Body that is truly present in the Blessed Sacrament of the altar and, at the same time, contradict Christ himself in his Mystical Body, present in the Church and in the ecclesial communion. Therefore, we can declare with no error whatsoever that if someone is in a state of mortal sin, he cannot and must not receive communion. It happens all the time: not only in the case described in the previous question, but in all cases in which there is an objective rupture with what God has willed for us. This is by definition the bond that is established among the various sacraments. Therefore we have to be very cautious about an immanentist understanding of the Sacrament of the Eucharist, that is, an understanding based on an extreme individualism. Specifically, we have to guard against believing subjectively that it is possible to be in communion with Christ and to keep God's commandments outside of the ecclesial communion, thus subordinating to one's own needs or tastes the reception of the sacraments or participation in the ecclesial communion.

The key to this whole problem, for some commentators, is the "desire to receive sacramental communion", as though the mere desire were already a right. For many others, communion is only a way of expressing membership in a community; it is the manifestation of a feeling of belonging to a group, which in turn involves many other feelings connected with it, such as the sense of identity, group pride, or fear of exclusion. Nevertheless, the Sacrament of the Eucharist cannot be considered reductively as an expression of a right or of a communal identity: the Eucharist cannot be a "social feeling"!

Often it is suggested that the decision to approach Eucharistic Communion should be left up to the personal conscience of the divorced and remarried. This argument is also an indicator of a problematic concept of "conscience" that was already rejected by the Congregation for the Doctrine of the Faith in 1994. Before approaching the altar to receive communion, the faithful know that they must examine their conscience, which also obliges them to *form* their conscience continually and, therefore, to be passionate in their *search for the truth*. In this very appropriate dynamic, obedience to the Magisterium of the Church is no burden at all but, rather, an aid in finding the much-desired truth about one's own good and the good of one's neighbors.

Question: One of the major challenges that come to light here is the relation between "doctrine" and "life". It has been said that, without changing the "doctrine", it is necessary now to adapt it to "pastoral reality". This adaptation would even imply that doctrine and pastoral praxis can in fact proceed along different paths. But does this not run the risk of presenting a very impoverished view of Christian doctrine? And, most importantly, is it possible to have a deeper pastoral vision without a more in-depth understanding of doctrine?

Cardinal Müller: This is another misunderstanding, as though doctrine were a theoretical system reserved to a few specialists in theology. No. Doctrine, in addition to the Word of God, gives us life and the most authentic truth about it. We cannot profess doctrinally that "Jesus Christ is Lord" and then not do his will. Christ is the way, the truth, and the life (cf. Jn 14:6): separating life from doctrine is like trying to separate Christ as Son of God from Christ as Savior. The split between life and doctrine is part of the Gnostic dichotomy. As is separating justice and mercy, God and Christ, Christ himself as Lord and as Shepherd, or separating Christ from the Church. There is only one Christ. Christ is the guarantee of the unity between the Word, doctrine, and one's own profession of the faith. Any Christian knows that only through sound doctrine can we attain life everlasting.

These theories that you mention seek to make Catholic doctrine a sort of museum of Christian theories; a sort of reservation that would be of interest only to a few specialists. Life, on the other hand, would have nothing to do with Jesus Christ, as he is and as the Church shows him. Basically, the Christian heritage would thus be transformed into a new, politically correct civil religion, reduced to a few values that are tolerated by the rest of society. This would achieve the disgraceful goal of some people: to sideline the Word of God so as to be able to manage all of society ideologically.

Jesus did not come into the world to expound a few simple theories that pacify consciences and, ultimately, leave things as they were without altering the "status quo". Jesus recreated creation by preaching a conversion that is possible for everyone, since he has already defeated sin definitively: he gave us the indicative as the basis for the imperative! This is why an authentic Christian life is so demanding, since it involves a personal commitment to change one's own conduct, without easy compromises between revelation and the world, without conforming oneself to a false anthropology. One cannot go to Church in the morning and to the brothel in the afternoon, as a sort of schizophrenic synthesis between God and the world, as though one could live in the "house of the Lord" in the morning and in the "house of the devil" in the afternoon.

The message of Jesus is a new life. If someone reasons and lives according to the parameters that you presented in your question, separating life and doctrine, not only does he deform the doctrine of the Church and transform it into an idealist pseudo-philosophy, he also deceives himself. That is not the doctrine of the Church. The *Catechism* outlines the new life of a Christian as a sort of unity between "believing in God", "praying to God", "celebrating God's life", and "living according to God's commandments". Living as a Christian, therefore, is living according to faith in God. To falsify this pattern is to make a foolhardy compromise between God and the devil.

Question: In order to defend the possibility of a spouse "redoing his life" with a second marriage (during the lifetime of the first spouse), some statements from the Fathers of the Church have been cited that seem to be along the lines of a tolerance for these new unions. What value do these statements of the Church Fathers have, and what patristic tradition supports the Catholic doctrine on this point? Earlier you mentioned Saint Augustine, but could you be a little more specific, so as to shed light on this aspect?

Cardinal Müller: The patristic writings developed in complete conformity with the Word of God, as it appears in the Bible. For Catholic theology, this connection between Scripture, tradition, and the Magisterium is fundamental. With respect to the specific problem you mention, it is certain that in connection with patristic writings we can find various interpretations and adaptations to everyday life, but there is no statement by the Fathers that tends to accept placidly a second marriage while the first spouse is alive. It is certain that in the Christian East there was confusion between the civil legislation of the emperor and the laws of the Church, which gave rise to a different praxis that in certain cases led to allowing divorce. But under the guidance of the pope, the Catholic Church over the course of the centuries has developed another tradition, which is specifically recorded in the current Code of Canon Law and in the rest of Church's regulations. In this theological and juridical heritage, we observe a legislator's intention that is clearly contrary to any attempt to secularize marriage. The same thing happened in various Christian contexts in the East.

Occasionally I have detected how a few accurate citations from the Fathers have been

selected and taken out of context in order to
support in this way the possibility of a divorce
and a second marriage. Methodologically, I
do not think that it is correct to isolate a text,
remove it from its context, turn it into a dis-
connected quotation, and break it off from the
overall framework of tradition. All theological
and magisterial tradition must be interpreted
in the light of the Gospel: with reference to
marriage, we rely on several absolutely clear
sayings of Jesus Christ himself and also on the
constant tradition of the Magisterium of the
Catholic Church, above all of the Council of
Trent and the Second Vatican Council, along
with the recent postconciliar development
summed up in the apostolic exhortation *Familiaris consortio*. I do not think it possible to have
an interpretation different from the one spelled
out thus far by tradition and the Magisterium
of the Church without being unfaithful to the
revealed Word.

It is certain, on the other hand, that dogma
develops and is evolving, but it is also certain
that it does not do this in a way that contra-
dicts basic principles. There is, for example, a

historical development that over the centuries led to the dogma of the Immaculate Conception, but after the proclamation of this dogma there can be no development that would conclude or affirm the contrary.

Question: In other words, there can be no development of dogma that finally leads us to deny dogma itself.

Cardinal Müller: That is correct. Let us take another example, the dogma of the Assumption of Mary: once it has been formulated and proclaimed, emphasizing very concretely the assumption of Mary in her body as well, it is not possible to conclude that this is a mere metaphor by alleging a supposed "continual development of dogma". We also know that marriage is indissoluble. It is possible to understand this more deeply and to explain it accordingly; it is possible also to discuss the conditions for it, but it is not possible to assert the contrary! In that case, we would be dealing, not with a development of dogma, but rather, as John Henry Newman said, with the corruption thereof.

Question: I would like to turn again to the specific topic of the challenges of the family. One of its major challenges is decided in the field of education. Pope Francis referred also to this challenge in his recent encyclical Evangelii gaudium *(no. 70) and returned to it later. The situation has been described as an "educational emergency". What difficulties do we encounter today in transmitting the things that make our children's lives great and beautiful? What in fact caused educational praxis to lose its impact and parents and teachers to lose their appeal and conviction in their educational work?*

Cardinal Müller: Many instructors of religion and especially parents have lost a bit of their courage and clarity in presenting the Christian faith, becoming very insecure. They lack the real-life foundations and the intellectual capacity to present the Christian message clearly, coherently, and, above all, attractively. What is needed is more study of the sources of the Christian faith contained in the *Catechism*. For example, one cannot cite a Father of the Church and then radically drift off course in one's theological explanation because one knows neither the context nor the principles that guided the development of a particular dogma as it is contained in the *Catechism*. Someone who does that serves neither the truth nor the persons to whom he speaks but, rather, creates more doubts and uncertainties.

Question: A major, fundamental topic is the "generativity" of the family. Here, obviously, we come to the topic of the dramatic demographic decline in the traditionally Catholic countries in the West, but also, and most importantly, to the difficulty families encounter in perceiving their mission today of generating a new society by means of work, education, and the creation of intermediate associations, and so on. Why has this difficulty in understanding the "generativity" of the family come about?

Cardinal Müller: I have already noted earlier how the Holy Father has spoken about those families that, instead of having children and loving them, prefer to adopt dogs or cats because they cause fewer problems. "Companion animals", pets in general, cannot be the center of anyone's life or his point of reference. We are persons, and only another person can satisfy a person's aspirations: a personal relationship fits us! It is telling that today many people, in this depersonalized, frivolous world, have lost their confidence in the future, influenced and manipulated by the ideology of well-being and hedonism. They have been convinced that their only goal in life and the only thing that really counts is to strive to acquire as many of the world's riches as they can: to work so as to be able to take the next vacation or to have the best possible free time and then to enjoy as much as they can, without moral restrictions. This false ideology has destroyed families and has poisoned the joy of having children and dedicating oneself to them. How can we avoid this trap? We will have to go back to stating the obvious. We all received life through the gratuitous love of our parents: we were happy when we were loved with such generosity; when we give ourselves in this way, we are happy. All Christian marriages should give joyful witness to the fact that children are never a chore or a burden, even in the most complex situations of life, but rather a project based on confidence and an inexhaustible source of happiness.

Question: But perhaps behind these questions there is a radical lack of understanding of what marriage is. What does it mean that marriage is a sacrament, if it is natural for a man and a woman to unite in a stable manner with the intention of starting a family?

Cardinal Müller: The very notion of sacrament is going through a serious crisis today. This crisis shows modern man's serious inability to conceive of reality symbolically and, therefore, to understand his own life in depth. The reason for this should be sought in a certain mechanistic image of the world, which considers matter solely from the viewpoint of quantity and individual things from the viewpoint of their function. The result of this reductive philosophy is that man does not know how to see the material world and particular things as means to an end. So it is that man, wallowing in wonderful superficiality and frivolity, becomes incapable of perceiving the signs within him pointing to a universal horizon and to the foundation of all being. If a materially structured symbol can no longer be seen as a means, as a form expressing a transcendent reality, then the sacraments become unthinkable. In this respect, sacramental theology depends strictly on a clear perception of the "symbol" from the philosophical and ontological perspective.

In order to approach the sacraments, it is important to understand the close relationship between nature and grace. Enlightened by the living God, we are able to believe in the reality of a God who is Father: for love's sake, he created us in his image and likeness, so that we might establish a personal relationship with him as our origin, our end, and the substance of our life. We can also believe in the reality of the Son of God who became man for our sake: for love's sake, he gave us his own life on the Cross and in his Resurrection. Finally, we are able to believe in the reality of the outpouring of the Holy Spirit: for love's sake, he inspires us and divinizes us with his life. When we understand all these mysteries of salvation, for the sake of which God willed to establish a perpetual covenant to save mankind, we are also capable of understanding this natural reality which is marriage, as a covenant in the service of that salvation.

Christian marriage is one of the seven sacraments of the New Covenant. By "Christian marriage" we understand that communion of life and love between a baptized man and a baptized woman. This communion of their whole life is exclusive, personal, and entered into freely. But it is also a unique communion, higher than all other forms of human communion, since it reflects Christ's covenant with his Church, by which marriage comes to be an efficacious sign that communicates sanctifying grace: in the words of the Bull for the Union of the Armenians of the Council of Florence in 1439, which clearly set out the teaching of Ephesians 5:32, "the Sacrament of Matrimony is the sign of the union of Christ and the Church."

God is present in marriage in a sacramental manner that is real, concrete, visible, and palpable. In light of the Incarnation, the natural reality of marriage has been raised to the level of an efficacious sign of God's grace. We know that grace is not a simple favor that God does for us with no further consequences or a mere feeling; above all, it is a participation in the new creation, in the new world to which we have all been called and toward which we have already been journeying. This is why we say that marriage expresses the grace of the Incarnation: the grace received in marriage is not only an *actual* grace, in the sense that it might externally help the natural union between a man and a woman. Above all, a *sanctifying* grace is offered to us: the grace received in the Sacrament of Matrimony transforms us interiorly, both as individuals and as communities! How different everyday life would be for many married couples who are languishing in drab mediocrity if they were to discover what they already are! It becomes necessary to deepen one's faith.

We Christians know (but we should deepen our reflection on it) that the marriage of baptized persons who are incorporated into the Mystical Body of Christ has a sacramental character and is a supernatural reality. In my opinion, as a pastor with a passion for theology, one of the most serious pastoral problems currently is rooted in the fact that many people today judge marriage exclusively according to worldly, pragmatic criteria. Someone who thinks according to "the spirit of the world" (1 Cor 2:12) cannot understand the sanctity or the sacramentality of marriage! This is a challenge for us, the pastors and the faithful of our time.

On the other hand, we know that a mere "accommodation" of the reality of marriage to the world's expectations bears no fruit but, rather, is even counterproductive: the Church cannot respond to the challenges of today's world with a "pragmatic adaptation". We must again place our trust in the "Spirit which is from God, that we might understand the gifts bestowed on us by God" (1 Cor 2:12). Sacramental marriage is a witness to the power of grace that transforms the man and the woman and prepares the whole Church to be the Holy City, the New Jerusalem, the Church herself "prepared as a bride adorned for her husband" (Rev 21:2).

Rather than a facile "pragmatic adaptation", we are called to opt for the martyr's "prophetic boldness". With that we will be able to witness to the "gospel of the sanctity of marriage". A lukewarm prophet would seek, by means of an "adaptation" to the spirit of the age, his own sort of salvation but not the salvation that God alone gives. On the other hand, we all know courageous prophets who straightforwardly and humbly proclaim the "gospel of conjugal love", testifying by their own lives that their love has been purified, strengthened, and increased by sacramental grace. Perhaps some will object that this task, although quite lovely, is too complicated; as though it had been proposed only for a few "chosen" individuals or "experts" in pastoral care to the family: we should recall here that all spouses, through the Sacrament of Matrimony, share in the definitive and irrevocable love of God. How can anyone fail to realize that this is the sacramental nature of matrimony? Every married couple who places God at the center of their conjugal life discovers with joy and amazement that their love is nourished every day and grows. Perhaps without even realizing it, they become witnesses of God's faithful love for all those around them, chiefly for their own children.

Question: Within the framework of the upcoming synod, the figure of Saint John Paul II comes to mind. In the homily at his canonization, Pope

Francis recalls that he was the "pope of the family". What does this mean? More specifically: Do the doctrine and magisterial teaching of John Paul II on the family continue to be relevant? Have his great insights really been put into practice? And above all: Is what Saint John Paul II left us as his teaching about marriage and the family really fresh and alive? Is it of any interest? Is it still up to date?

Cardinal Müller: Pope Francis declared Saint John Paul II "the pope of the family". Since he is patron of the family, this pope's extraordinary magisterial teaching on the family stands out. I would like to bring up here his brilliant "theology of the body" and all his teachings, especially the ones collected in his apostolic exhortation *Familiaris consortio*, which are an inexhaustible source for discovering the value of the human person and of the family. I consider this doctrine of Saint John Paul II to be a remedy for many of the defects that we have detected and denounced.

We judge a particular thing by its fruits: What are the effects of a mistaken concept of married life together? The reality is striking:

the "orphans of divorce", the disorientation of our young and not-so-young people, the falling birth rate in most wealthy countries, and, most importantly, the collapse of Western society, especially in Europe or in America. What future are we building for the next generations? The possibility of total collapse looms. We have to change course! The Church's doctrine on the family is precisely the remedy we need to save us from a predictable disaster.

Question: Saint John Paul II was a true friend of young families. During his entire priestly life, he assisted many couples in their first years of marriage. Today the problem arises of how to help these families. We know that most divorces and family breakdowns occur in the first five years of marriage. It is the period in which the couple faces the task of raising their first child (or, sometimes, tries unsuccessfully to do so) and many crises and difficulties arise with their respective families, a time when many difficulties in living together come to light. How does the Church make herself present in those first years? How can the Church's doctrine sustain the hope of these marriages?

Cardinal Müller: We have to go back to insisting on catechesis before marriage. Many times we detect the false ideas that we have just expounded in those young couples who come to our parishes to be married. It impresses me to see them so filled with high hopes and convinced of the depth of their love; and I am saddened that later on a large percentage of them will eventually break up irremediably. No one has given them emotional formation in what marriage means, both as a natural reality and as a grace. They do not realize that this secularized, materialistic, and hedonistic society has insistently told them in all the media and in every way that marriage is merely egotism for two, mutual selfishness. As a pastor, I tell myself: This cannot be! Someone will have to present the truth to them! Someone will have to open their eyes and tell them that they have been cruelly deceived by a false anthropology that leads only to disaster! On the other hand, though, how are we to do this? Surely, regardless of what pastoral means we employ, we must first of all keep very clearly in mind the fact that the solution is precisely to point out the false understanding of the human being—of his origin, end, and objectives—that they take as their starting point. The means that we use to do this will depend on the specific case, but above all we will have to speak to them about the authentic love and the concrete plan that Christ has for them.

Considering again the relation that exists between doctrine and life, I would say that the remedy for this situation is in living doctrine. "What is man?" we must ask continually. We have to be very careful, because all sorts of disasters follow from a false definition of man and his destiny, from an apparently "doctrinal" question. If we give a false definition of man, there are terrible consequences. If we obscure the fact that man must define himself in his relationship with God, the origin and end of the person, the result is absolute immanentism: a dead end in which man sees himself obliged to perfect himself by created means alone, among which sexuality appears as an idol. On the other hand, if contemporary man learns anew to see his life in the light of grace, he will be capable of rediscovering the supernatural vocation that gives meaning to the whole person: he will realize that he was created for something higher, for an infinite destiny and that the means for reaching that goal matter.

By the way, I think that the delusion today is rooted in this blending of a call to live solely by the means that the finite, worldly dimension has to offer with the offer of an infinite vocation. This blending eventually leads to confusion between the means and the end. In contrast, if I interpret my whole life in light of the Cross and Resurrection of Christ, I realize that I truly can face any difficulty that life may send my way. Then I can cope with sickness, old age, loneliness, rejection, widowhood, moments of discouragement or anger with one's spouse, or the challenge of having children, since they do not always turn out to be a joy for their families. It is important for me to ask myself constantly: Why am I doing this or that? What motivates my life? There is one answer that expresses a full meaning: I do this because I am responsible to the crucified and risen Christ.

Question: In his interview for La Civiltà Cattolica, *Pope Francis told us: "I see the Church as a field hospital after battle." Certainly, the Church must appear like that for the family: the place where their wounds can be healed, where they can receive warmth, closeness, and nearness. How should the "field hospital" Church act in the parishes, movements, family counseling centers, and so on? And how can she make sure that her action is not reduced to that of a psychologist or therapist? How can the Church do this so that the essential, ecclesial features of her activity emerge?*

Cardinal Müller: The image of a field hospital is very beautiful. Nevertheless, we cannot manipulate the pope by making this image an expression of the whole reality of the Church. The Church per se is not a healthcare institution: the Church is also the Father's house. Jesus suffered for our sake, and we can unite our sufferings with those of Christ. We know also that in this earthly life we cannot heal all the wounds that exist. When someone has seen a spouse or a child die, this causes a wound that cannot be overcome entirely. This wound will always remain there, with a scar forming over it, more or less: like the wounds of Jesus, which remain even after his Resurrection, so that we might know that God alone will definitively heal all wounds at the end of time. The Church, on the other hand, is called in this world to give the hope that enables us to endure life patiently with the wounds that we accumulate.

It is neither lawful nor right, for example, for a layman or a priest to tell someone who is suffering because she has been abandoned by her spouse, "Well, now you can marry someone else." That does not help, since this person is still wounded by the abandonment that she has suffered, and, as we know, a wound is not healed simply by covering it up or even by denying that it exists. One is not healed by merely trying to "start over from zero". One is healed by offering up to Christ the wound that one has suffered, by fighting the good fight of the faith (cf. 1 Tim 6:12).

Only at the end of time, as the Book of Revelation says, will God "wipe away every tear from our eyes" (cf. Rev 21:4). Only at the end of time will all our sorrows be over. Moreover, the wound of someone who suffers from abandonment by his spouse because of divorce is not the only wound we can suffer on this earth.

There are many different kinds, and even some that are just as serious or more so. Therefore, it is a sign of maturity to recognize that we cannot overcome all sufferings, that there is no "earthly paradise". It is not other people's job to promote the vain illusion of a this-worldly paradise, nor is it the Church's task.

Question: I would like to mention here also the witness of so many holy marriages. A book was published recently in Spanish with the title Esposos y santos *with portraits of various married couples who attained holiness in the perfection of their family life. Does this witness continue to be valid and relevant? What value do they have for our society? What do holy marriages help us to understand?*

Cardinal Müller: It is true that we do not have many canonized married couples. Perhaps the root cause is not that they are numerically fewer but, rather, that it is more difficult to prove their holiness. It may be that the Church has to work more in this direction. It is certain that we all are acquainted with the witness of many saintly married couples who are not officially recognized as such, not canonized. They were normal people, like so many Christians, who joyfully lived a Christian life. There have been and there are today many of these marriages, and the reason for this is found in matrimony itself, since it is a sacrament for sanctifying persons. The sacramental grace of matrimony not only helps the couple live their everyday life with gladness: it also helps bring them to share in the holiness of God. Therefore, matrimony is a sacrament, not a mere blessing. But surely it is also a good idea to offer to our young people testimonies of conjugal sanctity. In particular, we should offer the example of the Holy Family, the original model of a holy marriage.

Question: In Evangelii gaudium, *Pope Francis spoke to us about the problem of poverty and about the social problem. This is a subject that perhaps, as we pointed out earlier, should be correlated in the first place with personal relationships: the greatest poverty is the absence of authentically human relationships and the loneliness in which many, many people find themselves today (now, ironically, in the era of communications). How can we foster a true, integral development starting with the family? How can we foster the relational virtues specific to the family?*

Cardinal Müller: In the family we learn that man is eminently relational. Without the relationships that we establish over the course of life, in a wide variety of forms, there is no personal enrichment. This is so because the person is, by definition, a being in relation. Therefore, when someone has not experienced a normal family, he suffers from a serious relational poverty. The family is a domestic church or a living cell that makes the social organism as a whole function. To live in the bosom of a family in this way assures one's adequate incorporation into a larger society.

A good family policy understands that families need resources in order to achieve the goal of being "living cells of society". Families, especially large ones, have need of material resources in order to feed and educate their children. They have to rely on sufficient assistance to be able to have access to health care and to all the things that are consistent with a life lived with dignity: access to education, to the intellectual dimension, and to a moral life—basic things that clearly show that man was created in the image and likeness of God.

Catholic theology has condemned oppositions between the person and society or between individualism and collectivism. These extremes spring from a Gnostic dualism between soul and body, between Christ as the Head of the Church and the Church as the Body of Jesus Christ, between ecclesiology and Christology. It is the same false dualism that many people posit between a this-worldly existence without God and a path toward transcendence. All these elements make sense only if they are seen as complementary. This is why we can speak about poverty as Pope Francis does, without falling into an ideological perspective.

The Catholic proposition has always been able to avoid extremes, extreme alternatives: either God or the world, either God or man, either the Cross or the Resurrection, either the soul or the body. Life is immanent and contains immanent purposes, but we know, too, that the ultimate, transcendental purpose is the one that crowns all existence. Communism and *laissez-faire* capitalism offered a paradise on earth, in opposition to the authentic heavenly paradise that every Christian aspires to. We make of our lives an attempt to achieve full harmony between things that seem irreconcilable, between the two poles, because we perceive that there is no real contradiction between them: precisely because we are oriented toward the heavenly paradise, we can take full responsibility for our duties toward creation, toward the men and women of the whole world, toward societies, toward the different cultures and toward any form of poverty whatsoever. True humanism is theocentric. Therefore, instead of thinking about life in terms of oppositions, we have to learn from Christian humanism to live joyfully and harmoniously both sides of the same coin.